Bugs, Beware!

John Manos and Lisa Klobuchar

Illustrated by John Kanzler

Contents

Rigby

A Harcourt Achieve Imprint

www.Rigby.com

1-800-531-5015

Chapter 1   Needed and Needy

It's just another sunny morning at the **bog.** Croaking fills the swamp's steamy air, snakes slither in the shadows, and dragonflies patrol the skies. Near the ground, looking like a clump of wide-open little mouths lined with spiny teeth, is a small plant. Attracted by the sweet smell that rises from the little mouths, a shiny green fly zooms in close, lands, and walks slowly between a pair of gaping jaws. One lucky resident of the bog is about to enjoy a meal. If you're thinking it's the fly, well, you'd better think again.

The fly brushes against two hairs inside the little mouth of the plant. Slowly the plant's "jaws" close firmly on the fly. At first the fly struggles, but it's already too late. The more the unlucky insect wiggles, the tighter the plant's jaws clamp down.

It's breakfast time for a little **carnivorous,** or meat-eating, plant called the Venus flytrap.

Slowly but surely this plant traps a bug.

3

We need plants. In fact, humans and other animals owe their very lives to plants. We cannot survive without two very important things that only plants can produce—food and oxygen.

To carry out this important work, all plants—tall grasses, twisted pines, feathery palms, prickly cactuses, and the odd-looking Venus flytrap—need the same basic things to survive: water, sunlight, air, and **minerals.**

So, if all plants do the same job using the same things, why does one plant look so different from another?

 Tall trees block most of the sunlight from these ferns, but they're growing just fine—they don't need a lot of light to survive.

The Venus flytrap has adapted to live in a damp environment with poor soil.

Plants **adapt,** or change, to help them meet their needs in their **environments.** Different environments (places where plants live) provide different amounts of the things plants need to survive. For example, desert environments are sunny, but they provide very little water, so the fleshy stems and thick skin of cactuses and other desert plants have adapted to store water. On the other hand, the floor of a tropical rain forest has plenty of water, but little sunlight. Under no circumstances could cactuses grow there because they need a lot of sunshine and because the wet conditions of a rain forest would damage their roots.

Chapter 2 Meat-Eating Plants

The minerals that plants need are present in soil, and most plants soak them up through their roots, but some plants grow in places, such as swamps, where the soil doesn't have enough minerals. Most plants can't live in places like that, but a few plants have adapted in amazing ways to get the minerals they need from poor soil. They eat *animals!*

Carnivorous plants don't eat elephants, alligators, or people, but they do eat many types of insects and spiders, and some meat-eating plants can capture and eat tiny birds, rats, frogs, and even small monkeys!

Most plants could not live in this poor soil, but these pitcher plants grow beautifully.

These carnivorous plants—butterworts and Venus flytraps—can live even where there aren't a lot of minerals in the soil.

There are more than 500 types of carnivorous plants found throughout the world, from tiny bladderworts that live in ponds to huge pitcher plants that can trap and **digest** jungle rats. Many types of carnivorous plants live in wetland environments, while others live in tropical rain forests. Because humans are destroying many of these environments, carnivorous plants are becoming more and more rare in the wild. Unfortunately, some have died out and become extinct while many others are rapidly coming close to extinction.

Warning: Dangerous Plants!

In most ways, carnivorous plants are like other plants. They are usually rooted in one place, they make their own food, and they have stems, flowers, seeds, and leaves. But unlike most plants, the leaves of carnivorous plants are adapted to trap and digest animals. The leaves of some meat-eating plants may spring shut when an animal touches them, or they may hold the **prey** in place with sticky liquids. The leaves of other carnivorous plants may form a deep, watery trap from which no prey can escape. Maybe warning signs should be put up near these plants, so unsuspecting bugs don't get too close!

Carnivorous plants' leaves adapt for their insect-eating lifestyle

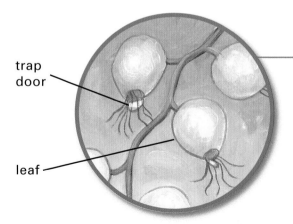

trap door

leaf

bladderwort

Hollow, balloonlike leaves suck tiny water animals inside, and a "trap door" shuts tight on unlucky prey.

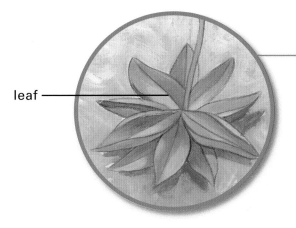

butterwort

leaf

Fleshy leaves make a goo that attracts insects, and then the leaves curve in to trap the insects.

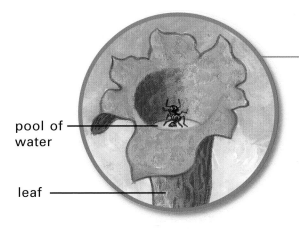

pitcher plant

pool of water

leaf

Folded leaf forms a tube-shaped trap, and a pool of water drowns prey.

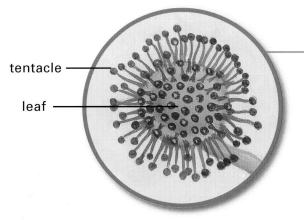

sundew

tentacle

leaf

Small round leaves produce sticky dew to attract prey, and the leaves' tentacles curl around prey to smother it.

9

Chapter 3

Venus Flytraps

What smells and looks like a sweet, white flower, but acts like a fierce shark? It's the Venus flytrap, of course. The Venus flytrap can attract, trap, and digest insects. To attract insects, the plant makes a sweet liquid called **nectar.** To trap insects, the Venus flytrap's leaves have developed folds down their centers, forming two halves that open and close like jaws. The edges of these jaws are lined with little brushes called **bristles.**

 Venus flytraps close more quickly on warmer days. Spider, watch out!

When an insect crawls between the plant's jaws for a sip of nectar, the insect's body touches hairs on the inside of the leaf. Then the two halves of the leaf clamp down on the insect, but this leaf trap does not snap shut quickly. If it did, it might warn the insect, and then the insect could get away. Instead, the unfortunate bug finds itself staring through the bristles of the leaf edges, like a prisoner looking through the bars of a jail cell!

 Some people raise Venus flytraps in their homes or in greenhouses. This will keep the plants from becoming extinct.

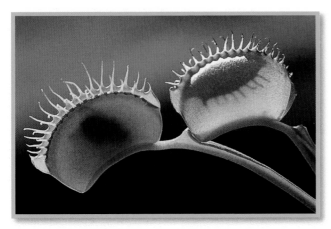

Look closely at the trap on the left. You can see the shadow of a trapped fly. The fly will soon become a healthy mineral soup for the plant.

Since the Venus flytrap doesn't have teeth for chewing, like you do, how can it eat an insect? Instead of chewing, the Venus flytrap squeezes the two halves of its leaf tighter and tighter until the insect can't breathe. The insect dies, and the leaf trap fills with a sticky liquid that breaks up the soft parts of the insect's body and turns them into a mineral soup that the plant can absorb.

Venus flytraps are astonishing plants, but they are becoming more and more rare. They are found only in a very small area of the world—in the swamps along the coasts of North and South Carolina. People keep draining the swamps and building on the land where Venus flytraps live. In the past, people have also collected too many of these plants to grow in their homes and didn't leave enough growing outside in their natural environment. Now Venus flytraps are protected, so if you want one in your home, you have to buy it from a **greenhouse,** where you will get instructions on how to properly care for this unusual plant.

How a Venus Flytrap Catches Prey

1

The trap is set. With its "jaws" wide open, the plant waits for an insect to show up.

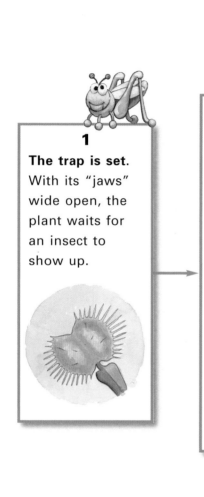

2

The prey moves. Looking for a meal, an insect crawls between the leaf halves and touches one of the hairs. Will the trap be sprung?

If the insect stays still and doesn't touch another hair within about 20 seconds, nothing happens. The insect lives!

If the insect touches a second hair, both halves of the leaf slowly fold over the insect. Uh-oh! The insect might become mineral soup.

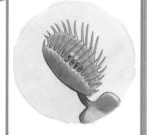

If the insect is too small to be a good meal, it can crawl between the plant's bristles and escape.

3
Will it get the big squeeze?
This depends on how big the insect is.

If the insect is too large to get away and it continues to touch the plant's hairs, the trap closes tighter and tighter.

4
Dinner is served!
The trap keeps squeezing, and the insect stops breathing as the leaf fills with sticky liquid.

5
Time to eat again!
After about two weeks, all of the insect's soft parts have dissolved. Now the plant gets ready for another meal!

Chapter 4 Bladderworts

Imagine you are a small water flea, just minding your own business in your small corner of a pond, when suddenly you smell something sweet—could it be food? You paddle quickly toward the smell and discover that it's coming from a small **sac** (like a pocket) with a round opening, not much bigger than yourself. Are there goodies inside the sac?

 Don't be fooled by these harmless looking plants! Bladderworts are deadly to small water insects.

Many types of bladderworts have lovely, colorful flowers. Some of them look like orchids.

As you move closer, your legs brush against a tiny hair in the opening, and before you can say "Dinner!" the sac gets bigger. A rush of water sucks you in, and a "door" snaps shut over the opening. Wildly you swim around and around, looking for a way out, but the door is shut tight. You've been trapped by a carnivorous plant called a bladderwort, and the worst is yet to come.

The water begins to drain slowly out, and since you're a water flea and water fleas need water to stay alive, you're in big trouble. After all the water drains out, you die, and tiny living things called **bacteria** in the bladderwort's sac start to turn you into a mineral soup.

Most bladderworts float in ponds and have many long stems that hang down into the water. These stems are covered with tiny balloonlike traps, called **bladders,** the largest of which are only about the size of this letter *o*. Hairs around the opening of each bladder cause the bladder to suddenly fill with water when prey touches them, and then the prey is sucked into the bladder so quickly that you can't even see it happen.

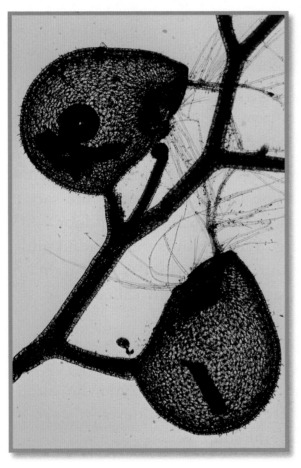

 The bladderwort trap at the top (no bigger than the head of a pin) has just caught a tiny water creature. Can you see it inside the bladder?

Never can the traps digest hard **skeletons,** so these parts of the bladderwort's victims stay with the plant forever. Over time, more and more of these leftover body parts collect inside the traps, so if you cut open a bladderwort's bladder, you can see the undigested remains of everything it has ever eaten!

 Bladderworts can catch many animals in a short time. People once found a bladderwort that had 90 traps holding 270 tiny creatures!

Chapter 5   Sundews

As sunlight shines over the earth, little drops of moisture twinkle on the ends of the pretty red hairs of a sundew plant. The drops smell sweet to a small moth flying nearby. Down the moth flies, landing on the plant to enjoy a sip of this delicious juice. But what's this? These drops are sticky. The moth's wings and feet get stuck, and it can't escape!

 A sundew looks almost like any other pretty flower, but it can be a death trap for a bug!

As the moth struggles, more sticky fluid oozes from the hairs of the plant, and these shiny red hairs slowly curl around the trapped moth, like fingers forming a fist. Soon the moth is completely covered in sticky goo, and, unable to breathe, it dies. Once the sundew has digested this yummy meal, the leaf unfolds, and the moth's leftover body parts blow away in the wind.

 Because insects breathe through tiny holes on the sides of their bodies, they die when these holes get covered in sticky sundew goo.

Sundews grow all over the world. Some sundews are tiny and trap only small insects, but others have leaves that are up to three feet long. These giant sundews (found mainly in Africa and Australia) can even capture small animals such as mice and birds, but these animals are usually strong enough to get away and rarely become a sundew's dinner.

 Those red and green plants in front look like a fancy kind of grass, but they are actually long-leaf sundews.

Interestingly, sundews seem to be very smart plants. They aren't fooled by twigs falling on their leaves and will wrap themselves only around insects or small animals. And here's something really creepy: If a piece of food such as a dead insect or a tiny piece of raw meat is placed close to a sundew, the plant will slowly stretch out its leaves and try to wrap its leaves around it—just as you might reach for a tasty snack!

Sundews "know" not to reach out for things they can't eat—like twigs or sand. They'll wait patiently for that tasty bug!

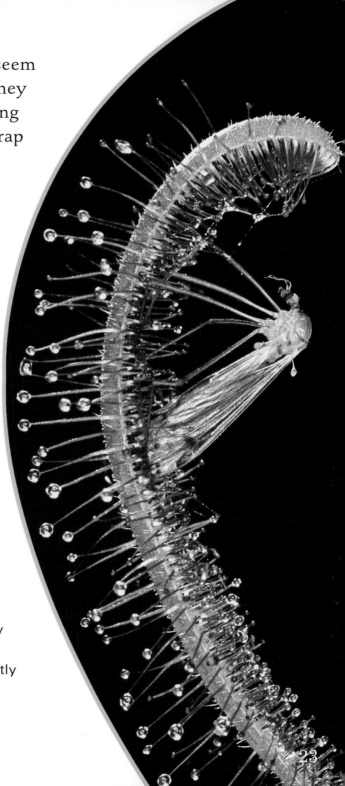

Chapter 6

Pitcher Plants

In places all over the world, you can find the tube-shaped pitcher plant hanging from vines and sprouting from the ground. The leaves of pitcher plants look like tall, slender, brilliantly colored water pitchers. At the bottom of these pitchers is a small pool of rainwater and a special liquid that dissolves the prey. An animal that gets trapped in the pitchers first drowns and then dissolves, providing a yummy meal for the plant.

Don't these pitcher plants look like they are opening their mouths and ready for lunch?

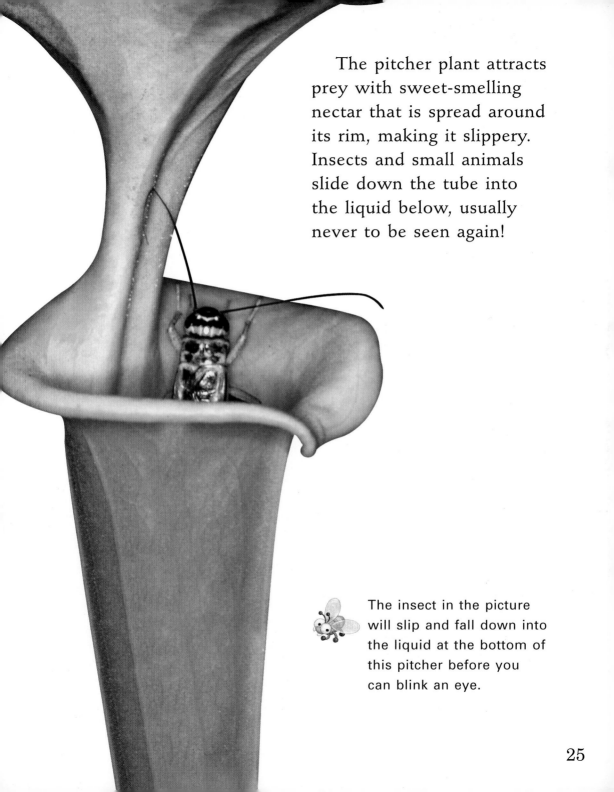

The pitcher plant attracts prey with sweet-smelling nectar that is spread around its rim, making it slippery. Insects and small animals slide down the tube into the liquid below, usually never to be seen again!

The insect in the picture will slip and fall down into the liquid at the bottom of this pitcher before you can blink an eye.

Even if the insect manages to crawl out of the water in the bottom of the plant, it's unlikely that it will be able to climb up the sides of the pitcher because tiny hairs and sharp teeth on the inside of the pitcher point in only one direction—downward. And if a determined insect does manage to climb past the slippery hairs and pointed teeth and reaches the top, it most likely will just slip on the plant's wet rim and fall to the bottom again. Once the insect drowns, the plant turns it into a mineral soup and soaks it up.

 Once this insect is dead, it will take the pitcher plant only two days to dissolve and eat it.

This huge pitcher can capture and eat animals that are larger than insects, such as this 3-inch-long frog.

People have found the bodies of small rats, birds, lizards, and even small monkeys inside the biggest pitcher plants. No one knows for sure how those animals got caught. They may have been curious or thirsty, or trying to eat the bodies of the insects that were already trapped inside the pitcher. Most animals larger than insects are strong enough to pull themselves free from a carnivorous plant. The animals that died in the pitcher plants may have been weakened by illness or old age and lacked the strength to escape.

Some animals found in pitcher plants are alive! Pitcher plants can dissolve only dead things, so sometimes frogs lay their eggs in the pools of water inside the pitchers. Some spiders and ants make their homes in pitcher plants and help the plants by acting as a cleaning crew, eating the leftovers from the pitcher plant's past meals, which otherwise might rot and poison the plant if they remain in the pitcher. There's also a special kind of pitcher plant that grows in California and Oregon—the "cobra plant." Though the cobra plant is deadly to most insects, certain types of moths and mosquitoes make their home in this particular pitcher plant. Would these bugs be safe around other carnivorous plants? They probably wouldn't, but these bugs seem quite snug in their cobra plant home!

 The spider helps the pitcher plant by removing leftover body parts, while the plant provides the spider with food and a safe home.

Chapter 7

Butterworts

Near a clear mountain stream, among little plants with pretty purple flowers like violets, a mosquito buzzes back and forth. The mosquito needs a rest, so it lands on a plant's leaves. Unluckily, this turns out to be a very bad move for the mosquito, because immediately the mosquito's legs are glued tightly to the leaf. This flower is not a violet—it's a butterwort! The rest stop turns out to be the end of the trip for this poor mosquito.

butterwort

violet

Many people can't tell this butterwort from a regular violet.

The entire surface of a butterwort's leaf is lightly coated with a layer of sticky goo, just like the ends of a sundew's leaves. This goo traps an insect while the leaf curls itself around it. Only very tiny insects are weak enough to not unstick themselves from this trap, but the butterwort is such a small plant that tiny insects make a delicious and filling meal for it.

The sticky goo that coats this butterwort has trapped its prey.

Not all butterworts look like violets.
Some look like other kinds of colorful flowers.

Butterworts live all over the northern half of the world. For butterworts to stay healthy, they need a lot of water and mild temperatures. If it becomes too hot or dry, the butterwort's sticky dew will dry up, and then it won't be able to feed itself. Many people like the butterworts that grow in Mexico because of their beautiful flowers and because they are such great bug catchers.

Chapter 8

A Different Kind of Pet

Some people have carnivorous plants at home. If you want your own carnivorous plant, just remember one important rule: Never take one from the wild! You can buy most types of carnivorous plants from greenhouses and companies that sell live plants and seeds.

Venus flytraps actually grow well in homes, and if you provide the plant with an environment similar to the one where it naturally lives, the plant will reward you by producing pretty leaves and growing for many years.

How about it? Would you like to have a pet Venus flytrap? If so, gather up the following items:

 • small plastic pot with holes in its bottom

 • soil mixture that is half **peat moss** and half sand

 • Venus flytrap plant

 • small plastic tray to put under the pot

 • small glass **terrarium**

 • **distilled** water

 • tweezers

 • live ants or flies

1. Fill the small plastic pot with a mixture of peat moss and sand. You can buy this mixture at the store or make it yourself. This special mixture is like the soil where Venus flytraps grow in the wild. Your Venus flytrap will get sick if you put it in the wrong kind of soil.

2. Carefully plant your Venus flytrap in the pot. Be sure that soil completely covers the plant's roots.

3. Put the small plastic tray inside your terrarium, and place the small plastic pot on top of the tray.

4. Gently water the soil around your plant, using only distilled water, which you can buy at the store (not water from the faucet). Then pour about an inch of water into the bottom of the tray, and be careful *not* to pour water on the plant's leaves.

5. During the months when your Venus flytrap is growing (April to September), put your terrarium near a sunny window that faces south or west. During the fall and the winter (October to March), move your terrarium near a colder window so that your plant can rest.

6. Use tweezers to put three or four *live* ants or flies (your plant will not eat a dead insect or a piece of meat) into the terrarium each month to feed your Venus flytrap. Clean the leaf traps after the plant's "jaws" open back up by gently blowing the insects' hard skeletons off the traps.

7. Don't ever play with the traps or set them off just for fun. Your plant is unable to eat while it resets the trap. Also, its leaves can open and close only a few times before they wear out and the plant must grow new ones.

Venus flytraps are small plants, and a healthy plant will only grow to about a foot in height and 5 inches wide with 4 to 8 "traps." Just follow these 7 steps, and you'll have a healthy, happy Venus flytrap for a long time. Have fun with your new pet!

Glossary

adapt change to fit in and survive in
an environment

bacteria very tiny and simple living things

bladder a small pouch filled with liquid
or gas

bog an area of wet, spongy ground;
a swamp

bristle short, stiff hair of some plants
or animals

carnivorous meat-eating

digest to break down food so the body
can use it

distill to make something pure by
heating it and letting it cool itself

environment all the surrounding things
that affect the growth of living things

greenhouse a building covered with a glass or plastic roof and sides, kept warm and full of light for growing plants

mineral a solid substance, usually dug from the earth; certain minerals help plants and animals grow

nectar sweet liquid found in many flowers

peat moss a dead, dried plant used as a potting mix

prey an animal that is hunted or seized for food by another animal

sac a baglike part in an animal or plant that usually contains liquid

skeleton the framework of bones inside the body

terrarium a glass container used for keeping plants indoors